Contents

KU-003-547

It's Christmas 4

Christmas is Special 6

To Bethlehem 8

Born in a Stable 10

An Angel Came 12

Follow the Star 14

King of Kings 16

Special Presents 18

Tell the Story 20

"Everybody Sing" 22

Remember the Star 24

Santa Has Been! 26

We Give Presents, Too 28

Family Fun 30

Glossary and Index 32

It's Christmas

Christmas morning
is very exciting.
We run downstairs
to see if Santa has
been. Our stockings
hang by the fireside.

Published in paperback in 2014 by Wayland

Copyright © Wayland 2014

Wayland
338 Euston Road
London NW1 3BH

Wayland Australia
Level 17/207 Kent Street
Sydney, NSW 2000

All rights reserved

Produced for Wayland by Calcium
Design: Emma DeBanks
Editor for Wayland: Victoria Brooker
Illustrations by Jennie Poh

British Library Cataloguing in Publication Data

Ganeri, Anita, 1961—
   Christmas is special. — (Special to me)
   1. Christmas—Juvenile literature.
   I. Title II. Series
   263.9'15-dc23

ISBN-13: 9780750283601

Printed in China

10 9 8 7 6 5 4 3 2 1

Wayland is a division of Hachette Children's Books,
an Hachette UK company.
www.hachette.co.uk

Christmas is Special

Christmas Day is so special because it is Jesus's birthday. Christians believe that God sent Jesus to Earth to help people live good, kind lives.

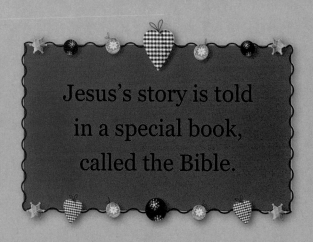

Jesus's story is told in a special book, called the Bible.

To Bethlehem

Long ago, there lived a woman called Mary. She was expecting a baby. Mary was married to Joseph. Mary and Joseph travelled to Bethelem to have the baby.

Little donkey!

Mary and Joseph went to
Bethlehem to be counted
and pay their taxes.

9

Born in a Stable

Bethlehem was very crowded. The only place for Mary and Joseph to stay was in a little stable. That night, Jesus was born! A star shone brightly above the stable.

An Angel Came

Nearby, some shepherds were watching their sheep. Suddenly, a bright light filled the sky. An angel appeared and told the shepherds that Jesus had been born.

Great news!

The angel told the
shepherds to be happy
because Jesus would
bring them peace.

Far away, three wise men saw a star shining in the sky. They followed the star across the desert to Bethlehem.

Far, far away

The star led the way to a great, new king – Jesus.

King of Kings

The star led the wise men to the stable where baby Jesus lay. The wise men knelt down before Jesus. They said he was the king of kings.

Praise him! Praise him!

Special Presents

The wise men brought presents for Jesus. One brought gold. One brought frankincense. One brought precious myrrh to heal.

Hallelujah! Hallelujah!

19

Tell the Story

Hooray!

The story of Jesus's birthday is called the nativity. At Christmas time, we act out this special story in church or school. We dress up as Mary, Joseph, shepherds, angels and wise men.

Hooray!

We sing special songs at Christmas to celebrate Jesus's birthday. These songs are called carols.

Away in a manger

Remember the Star

We put a star on top of our Christmas tree. It helps us to remember the star of Bethlehem. We put lots of lights and tinsel on the tree to sparkle like the star!

Sparkle and shine!

Santa Has Been!

It's Christmas morning and we can't wait! We run downstairs to see if Santa has been. There are so many presents under the tree.

Rustle, rustle, wow!

We Give Presents, Too

Getting presents is so exciting. But we like giving presents at Christmas, too. They help us to remember Jesus and how God sent him to Earth to show his love for the world.

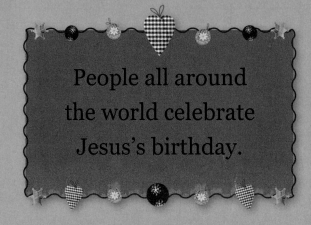

People all around the world celebrate Jesus's birthday.

What's inside?

29

Family Fun

Happy Christmas!

At Christmas, we have fun with our families and friends. A special Christmas dinner is a big treat. There are lots of yummy things to eat and Christmas crackers to make a loud BANG!

Glossary

Christians people who follow Jesus's teachings

desert a dry place with very little water

frankincense an oil that was once used as
a medicine

Jesus a holy teacher who lived thousands of years
ago. Christians believe that he is the son of God.

myrrh an oil that was once used as a medicine

taxes money people paid to the rulers of
their country

Index

angels 12–13, 21
Bethlehem 8–9,
    10, 15, 24
Carols 22–23
Christians 6
Christmas Day
    6, 30–31
Christmas
    morning 4,
    27, 28

Christmas trees
    24
God 6, 28
Jesus 6, 8, 10,
    12, 13, 15, 16,
    19, 21, 23, 28
Joseph 8, 9,
    10, 21
Mary 8, 9, 10, 21
nativity, the

20–21
presents 19, 27,
    28
Santa 4, 27
shepherds 12,
    13, 21
stars 10, 14–15,
    16, 24
wise men 15,
    16, 19, 21